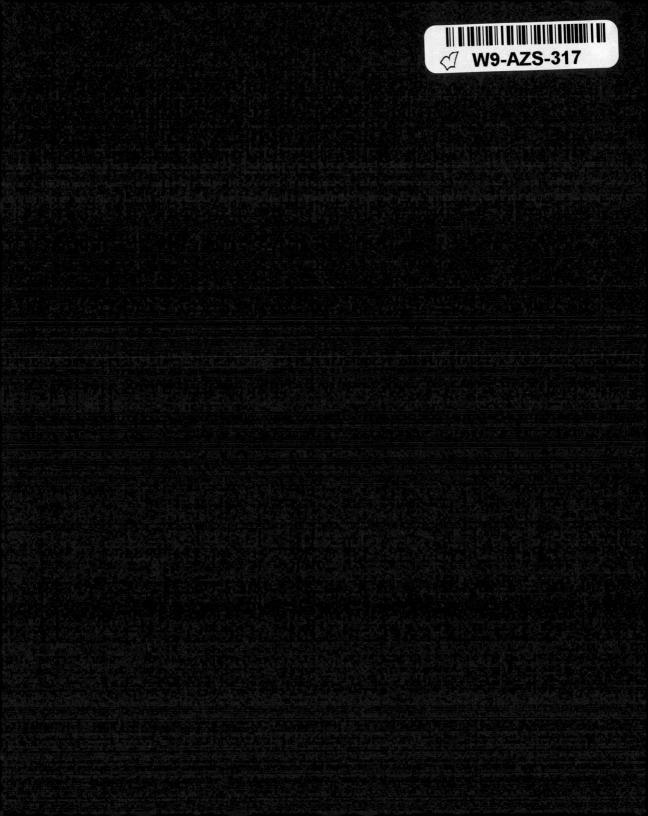

EARTHQUAKES

EARTHQUAKES

EARTHQUAKES

DAVID E. NEWTON

Franklin Watts
New York/Chicago/London/Sydney
A First Book

Photographs copyright ©:
U.S. Geological Survey/Photo Library, cover, 1, 4, 6, 11, 13, 16
(bottom right & left), 18, 21 (top, bottom), 23, 25 (top, bottom), 27, 36, 38, 46,
51 (top, bottom left & right), 58, 60, 61, 63; Wide World Photos, Inc., 7, 8, 14
(bottom), 42 (bottom), 53; Gamma Liaison/Lawrence Burr, 9; Frederick
McDonald Photography, 14 (top); Gamma Liaison/Rory Lysaght, 10, 15; Gamma
Liaison/Matthew Naythons, 16 (top); The Bettmann Archive, 19, 39; Historical
Pictures/Stock Montage, Inc., 20, 29; Gamma Liaison/Jay Dickman/Earthquake
Information Center, 37; UPI/Bettmann, 41, 42 (top); Cindy Charles/Liaison
International, 49; Gamma Liaison/Eric Sander, 50; Fundamental Photos/Richard
Megna, 52; Gamma Liaison/Torin Boyd, 54, 55.

Library of Congress Cataloging-in-Publication Data

Newton, David E.
Earthquakes / David E. Newton.
p. cm.—(A First book)
Includes bibliographical references and index.
Summary: Discusses how earthquakes happen, predicting and
measuring them, and some major earthquakes.
ISBN 0-531-20054-X   (HC, library binding)
ISBN 0-531-15664-8 (PB)
1. Earthquakes—Juvenile literature. [1. Earthquakes.]
I. Title. II. Series.
QE521.3.N49 1993
551.2'2—dc20
92-23291 CIP AC

CONTENTS

DEDICATION

Dedication for Lee Nolet with fond memories
and great appreciation for our friendship.

At Candlestick Park, baseball players Storm Davis and Lance Blankenship search the stands for family members minutes after the 1989 earthquake.

1

OCTOBER 17, 1989

Lee was very excited. How many eight-year-old boys get to see a World Series game in person? Yet, here he was, singing the National Anthem at Candlestick Park in San Francisco, California. In a few minutes, the game would begin. How lucky could a boy be?

But wait! What was that strange feeling beneath his feet? Did the stadium always shake like this when people clapped their hands? He didn't think so.

Suddenly he knew what was going on. An earthquake! He looked up. The roof of the stadium swayed back and forth. A piece of cement broke loose and fell to the ground. Some people screamed. Others ran for the exits. But most people just stood where they were. They did not realize what was happening.

In less than a minute, the shaking had stopped. The earthquake was over. No one was hurt. The stadium roof had not collapsed. People slowly understood what had happened. They felt very lucky to have survived the earthquake Nobody complained when the ball game was cancelled. They were alive and safe!

Not everyone, however, in the San Francisco Bay area was so lucky that October day in 1989. The Cypress Freeway that runs through Oakland was packed with drivers on their way home from work. Those drivers felt the roadway move, and then saw the upper deck of the freeway collapse in front of them. Forty-two people died on the freeway that day.

Not far away, a section of the Bay Bridge caved in. One driver did not see what had happened. Her car fell right off the bridge.

People who lived in the Marina District of San Francisco saw another horrifying result of the earthquake: fire. Gas pipes broke because the soft earth vibrated so violently it became a dust with the consistency of a liquid. Fires broke out in many buildings. Before long, roaring flames covered an area nearly a square mile (2.6 sq. km) in area.

Fires spread out of control in the aftermath of the 1989 San Francisco earthquake.

On the San Francisco-Oakland Bay Bridge, a section of roadway collapsed. The bridge remained damaged for months.

Thousands of people were driven from their homes.

The earthquake caused damage over a wide area. It actually began more than 50 miles (80 km) south of San Francisco. Its epicenter was under Loma Prieta peak, in the Santa Cruz mountains. The *epicenter* of an earthquake is the point where an earthquake begins.

The area around Loma Prieta is very different from San Francisco and Oakland. The region is very mountainous. It contains only a few cities and towns. In one way, that was lucky because relatively few people were killed.

But damage to buildings throughout the region was terrible. Three to four feet wide (.9 to 1.2 m) cracks opened in the ground. Houses slid off their foundations. Buildings collapsed into piles of bricks.

In just three cities near the epicenter—Santa Cruz, Hollister, and Watsonville—damage amounted to more than a billion dollars. More than 10,000 people lost their homes, and many would not find new homes for months. They lived in tents or outdoors.

The earthquake brought out the worst and the best in people. One landlord continued to charge rent on his Marina apartments even though no one could live in the damaged building. A restaurant owner charged $15 for a sandwich the night of the quake. A few people broke into damaged stores and stole as much as they could carry away.

But good stories were much more common than bad. One man walked the damaged streets of San Francisco giving away quarters. He wanted people to be able to call friends and relatives to say they were safe. Fire fighters risked their lives again and again going into damaged buildings to save injured people. An elderly woman lost her

This building in Santa Cruz, California, sustained severe damage.

After the earthquake, thousands were driven from their homes.
Many people salvaged only the possessions they could carry with them.

WIth too many fires for the fire department to handle, ordinary citizens were forced to take up hoses to save their own homes.

home and everything in it, but she went directly to the nearest hospital to work as a volunteer.

Perhaps the most inspiring story took place at the collapsed Cypress Freeway. Men and women worked twenty-four hours a day for more than a week looking for anyone who might still be alive. They were about to give up, but at the last moment they found a survivor, Buck Helm. Mr. Helm was injured, but still alive. He had survived in the rubble for an incredible eighty-nine hours after the earthquake. Mr. Helm was taken to the hospital where, a month later, he finally succumbed to his injuries and died.

The earthquake of October 17, 1989, lasted only fifteen seconds, but its effects lasted much longer. People in the San Francisco Bay area could still see reminders of the

The Cypress Freeway in Oakland, where the upper level of the highway collapsed on the lower level, sandwiching dozens of people in their cars.

quake a year later. Many buildings in the Marina District had still not been repaired. Landslides were still common in the mountains of Santa Cruz County. Many families still had not been able to replace homes lost in the earthquake. Some people had lost their businesses, and others were still out of work.

Traffic in and around San Francisco and Oakland had not yet recovered. Freeways that had been weakened by the earthquake were still closed as they had been weakened by the earthquake. They were too dangerous to drive on. The Cypress Freeway was completely torn down and may never be rebuilt.

But most of all, people still had memories. Lee finally got to see his World Series game, twelve days after it was cancelled. He would never forget that fifteen seconds of shaking. Other people would always remember the fires, the collapsing freeways, the open cracks in the earth, the loss of their home, or the death of a loved one.

2

THE EARTH MOVES

Earthquakes are nothing new to San Francisco. One of the great disasters of modern times was the San Francisco earthquake of 1906. That earthquake was more than ten times as powerful as the quake of 1989. In the minutes immediately following the 1906 earthquake, hundreds of people died and many buildings were destroyed. But far more damaging were the fires that soon began to burn. For three days, the fires raged through the city. When they finally burned out, the city of San Francisco had been destroyed.

The San Francisco Bay is just one of many areas around the world where earthquakes occur on a regular basis. Disasters like those in San Francisco are especially common in nations bordering the Mediterranean Sea and the Pacific Ocean, and across the middle of Asia. Records of these earthquakes go back at least 3,000 years. The most terrible earthquake ever recorded in terms of human life took place in China in 1556. More than 830,000 people were killed in that quake.

History contains many other horrible examples of the damage earthquakes can cause. In 1564, southern France

Early twentieth-century missionaries in Western China survey the ruins of an earthquake in the town of Liangehow.

A German engraving depicts the Lisbon eathquake of 1755.

was visited by a volcanic eruption and an earthquake at the same time. Seven towns were totally destroyed.

On November 1, 1755, an earthquake hit Lisbon, Portugal. The quake and the fires that followed took more than 60,000 lives. Effects of that earthquake were felt hundreds of miles away, killing and injuring thousands of people in Central Europe and North Africa.

A terrible earthquake struck Japan in 1891. Nearly 10,000 people were killed, 20,000 were injured, and more than 130,000 buildings were destroyed in the provinces of Mino and Owari.

Devastation caused by the 1886 earthquake that struck Charleston, South Carolina.

Maybe these stories make you feel safe if you live in Grand Rapids or Toronto or St. Louis. These cities are all away from earthquake zones. But scientists have learned that earthquakes can occur at any time in almost any place. In fact, small earthquakes occur every day. An average of ten per day are serious enough to shake the Earth, while about two a month are powerful enough to knock down buildings and injure people.

In 1886, for example, a terrible earthquake struck Charleston, South Carolina. Sixty people died, hundreds more were injured, and millions of dollars worth of property was destroyed. The quake was felt as far away as New York City, Chicago, and St. Louis. So, you see, earthquakes can strike almost anywhere.

Anyone who has lived through an earthquake can describe it for you. The ground moves slowly back and forth. You might feel as though you were on a boat. Or the ground may jiggle up and down.

Pictures swing back and forth on the wall. Water sloshes out of the dog's dish. Glasses rattle in the kitchen cabinet. Tall buildings sway back and forth. Sometimes you hear a roaring sound, like a freight train.

These signs of an earthquake are easy to see, feel, and hear. But what is happening in the earth itself?

Nearly all earthquakes occur along a fault. A *fault* is a place where two moving sections of the Earth's crust are pushing against each other with enormous pressure. When the crust on both sides of a fault moves, an earthquake may occur.

For example, San Francisco and Los Angeles lie along the San Andreas Fault. Land on the west side of the San

A section of the San Andreas Fault in California.

Andreas Fault is slowly moving toward the north. Land to the east of the fault is moving southward. During an earthquake, land on opposite sides of the fault can slide a meter or more past each other.

In some places you can actually see signs of a fault on the surface of the ground. For example, a fence may run straight and true for many meters on one side of a fault, but suddenly the fence ends where the fault cuts through the ground. You have to look one way or the other to see where the fence starts up again. The fence has been displaced by the Earth's movement along the fault.

Sometimes two sections of ground pull away from each other as they moved and large gaps in the ground open up. There are stories of buildings, people, and animals falling into these gaps, never to be seen again.

At other times two sections of Earth may push toward each other as they slide along. Then, one section may bend into an upside-down U shape. If the sections keep pushing, the upside-down U may break. Perhaps you have seen pictures of this change. The ground looks as though two giants had pushed on it from opposite sides.

Earthquakes cause damage in more than one way. As the ground trembles, buildings shake and sway. Walls and ceilings may cave in. The building itself may collapse. People are often trapped, crushed, injured, and killed.

Fire is another serious problem. Underground gas pipes often break, and a single spark can cause a terrible fire. One burning candle knocked over could do the same. Many times, the worst damage is not caused by the earthquake itself, but by the fires that follow.

The Alaska earthquake of March 27, 1964. The quake spawned tsunamis, which washed this boat into the center of the town of Kodiak (top), and destroyed virtually every structure along the northwest section of Resurrection Bay (bottom).

Earthquakes can also cause huge ocean waves called *tsunamis.* An earthquake may cause large sections of the ocean floor to move underwater causing huge landslides on the ocean bottom which can begin tremendous waves. At sea, these waves may not be very large. A boat riding on them might not even notice them because they travel deep below the surface. But as they approach shallow water, these waves spread out and begin to travel very fast. When they begin to meet the surface, they get much large, and by the time they hit shore, they can be more than 100 feet (30 m) high.

The Alaska earthquake of 1964 set off tsunamis in many directions. Some destroyed coastal towns in Alaska while others swept across the Pacific Ocean at 400 miles per hour (644 kph). They washed ashore in Canada, Washington, Oregon, and California. After traveling 4,000 miles (6,437 km), they still had enough force to destroy buildings and drown people.

Earthquakes are also often followed by landslides. The quakes open up cracks in the ground. Soil and rocks slide into the cracks. Sometimes the slides occur very slowly and they are hard to notice. Other times they happen all at once. Houses, buildings, farmlands, animals, and people may be swept away or buried by the slide.

Perhaps you can see why earthquakes are so feared. They come without warning, and they destroy property and lives in many ways.

3

WHAT CAUSES AN EARTHQUAKE?

What causes an earthquake? People have been asking this question for hundreds of years. Some of the earliest answers sound strange to us today. For example, some people once thought the Earth rested on a giant fish called Celebrant. People believed that as the fish moved around it shook the Earth and caused earthquakes.

The Greeks and Romans had another idea. They thought the inside of the Earth contained many large caves. From time to time, one of these caves would collapse, causing the Earth's surface to move and shake, producing an earthquake.

Gods and spirits have often been blamed for causing earthquakes. From the ancient Babylonians to the present day, some people have believed that earthquakes are a form of punishment. When people or cities or nations are bad, they are punished by an earthquake. The Romans believed they could prevent earthquakes, for example, by placing statues of Mercury and Saturn, two of their gods, in their houses.

Some early scientists thought that earthquakes were caused by natural explosions inside the Earth. The chemicals used to make gunpowder can be dug up from the ground. Perhaps these chemicals react with each other naturally, scientists said. The resulting explosions might set off an earthquake.

By the twentieth century, scientists had rejected all of these ideas. They had developed a modern theory of the way earthquakes occur. Their answer was based on the fact that the Earth had been very hot when it was first formed. Over millions of years, however, it cooled down, and as it cooled, it grew smaller and pulled inward. Perhaps you have seen what happens to an apple when it dries out—its skin breaks and becomes wrinkled. That is what happened to the Earth, many scientists believed. The mountains and valleys on the Earth's surface are like the wrinkles on the apple's skin. The oceans are valleys that became filled with water. Earthquakes occur when the Earth's "skin" shrinks and breaks apart.

This theory was not perfect, but when it was developed most scientists believed they were on the right track to explaining, earthquakes.

One scientist who disagreed with this theory was Alfred Wegener, a German *meteorologist* (a weather scientist). He proposed the idea that the Earth's continents are constantly moving. The movement of continents causes earthquakes and volcanoes, and creates mountain ranges and other familiar features on the Earth's surface, Wegener said.

Picture a lake in the middle of winter. You might see large chunks of ice floating on the lake. These islands of ice are likely to bump into each other from time to time. One chunk of ice may actually get pushed up on top of another chunk. Two chunks may rub sideways against each other.

Alfred Wegner, a meteorologist who first proposed the idea that the Earth's continents slide on plates, causing earthquakes and volcanoes.

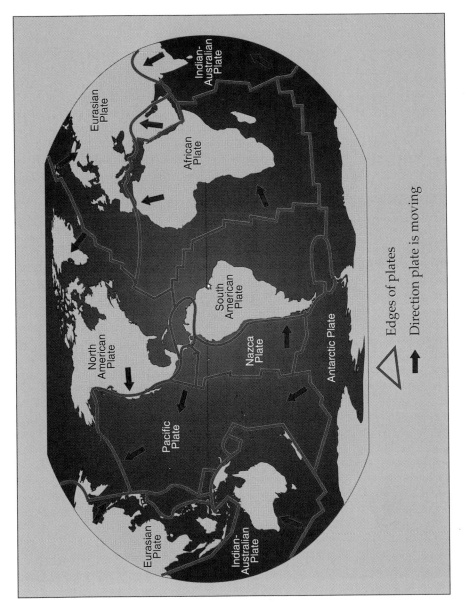

Plate Tectonics map.

Pieces of ice may break off.

The movement of ice on a lake resembles Wegener's idea of the way continents move on the Earth's surface. The continents move very slowly, seldom more than a half-inch (1 cm) a year. As the continents move, they may push up against each other, like chunks of ice on a frozen lake. The edge of one continent may slide up on top of another continent. Huge pressures can build up. When the pressures get too great, pieces of Earth may bend, slip, or break. When that happens, an earthquake occurs.

Most scientists laughed at Wegener when he proposed his theory in 1915. How could whole continents slide back and forth across the Earth's solid surface? One scientist said his idea was "an impossible hypothesis." Wegener's ideas were ignored by other scientists for nearly thirty years after he died in 1930.

By the 1960s, however, scientists had changed their minds. Research showed that the material under the Earth's continents was not solid! Instead, it was made of hot, liquidlike rock. The rock behaves very much like "silly putty." It slides around and changes shape very slowly.

When the liquid rock moves, so do continents and the ocean bottoms. The theory of "floating continents" was no longer such a silly idea. In fact, scientists soon had enough evidence to convince them that the idea was probably correct. The Earth's continents and ocean basins really do seem to be floating and drifting across the Earth's surface.

Today scientists have shown that the Earth's surface is made of nearly a dozen large and small *plates.* A plate is a large piece of the Earth's crust. Most plates hold one of the continents. The plate under the United States, Canada, and

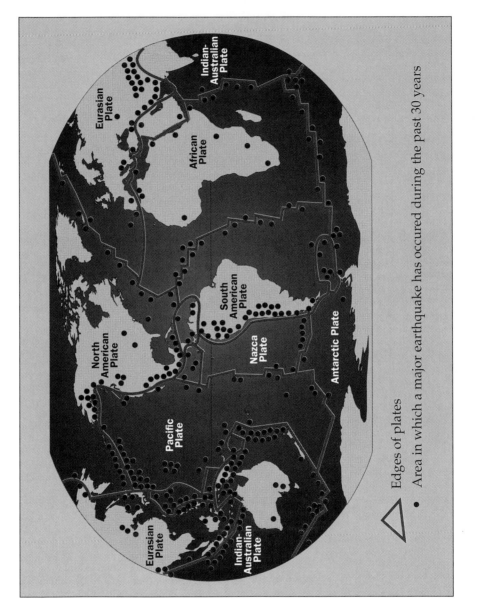

Eurasian Plate

Indian-Australian Plate

African Plate

North American Plate

South American Plate

Nazca Plate

Antarctic Plate

Pacific Plate

Eurasian Plate

Indian-Australian Plate

△ Edges of plates

• Area in which a major earthquake has occured during the past 30 years

Earthquake location map.

Mexico, for example, is called the North American Plate. Some plates lie beneath ocean basins. The Pacific Plate, for example, lies under the Pacific Ocean. Europe and part of Asia float on the Eurasian Plate.

Wherever two plates touch each other, earthquakes and volcanoes are common. In California, the North American Plate rubs against the Pacific Plate. The San Andreas fault lies on the boundary of these two plates. Many other faults lie on the same boundary. When the plates move, an earthquake occurs. The more they moves, the bigger the earthquake.

The theory of moving continents explains how 95 percent of all earthquakes occur. But some quakes occur in the middle of a plate, because they cannot be the result of two plates colliding with each other. How can these earthquakes be explained?

In some cases, an earthquake is caused by volcanic action. During a volcanic eruption, melted rock escapes from inside the Earth. It explodes and flows out the volcano during eruption. But the melted rock also pushes on rocks inside the volcano. This push sets off earthquakes in the ground around the volcano.

People can cause earthquakes too. Oil, chemical, and other industries sometimes dump liquid wastes into very deep holes in the earth. If the holes lie along a fault, earthquakes may follow. The liquid wastes may push against opposite sides of the fault. As the rock sections push apart, they may slide past each other more easily. The movement of the rock can set off an earthquake.

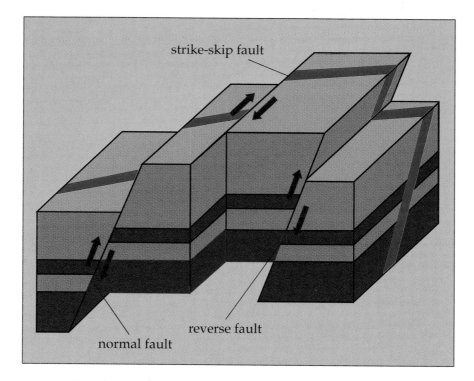

strike-skip fault

normal fault

reverse fault

There are three types of faulting (pictured above) that cause the majority of earthquakes. Normal faults (left) occur when two blocks of earth move apart and one block drops down. In a strike-skip fault (center) , the fracture in the earth extends straight down and the two blocks of earth slide past one another horizontally. Neither block of earth rises of falls. In reverse faulting (right), two blocks of earth strike together and one is forced underneath the other.

Water can have the same effect. The construction of a new dam may be followed by earthquakes if the water behind the dam seeps into the earth. The water causes sections of rock to push apart and slide against each other more easily. This movement can set off an earthquake.

4
MEASURING EARTHQUAKES

"Yesterday's earthquake measured 4.2 on the Richter scale."

People who live in earthquake zones are familiar with announcements like this one. The *Richter scale* is a way of measuring how powerful an earthquake is. The highest measurement ever recorded was 9.5. It was made during an earthquake in Chile in 1960. How does the Richter scale work?

The Richter scale measures waves caused by an earthquake. When an earthquake occurs, it pushes on rocks around the epicenter. Those rocks, in turn, push on other rocks around them. The "push" that started at the epicenter travels outward. It can travel for hundreds or thousands of miles.

You have probably seen a similar effect in water. Drop a stone into water. You can see the waves travel outward, away from the stone. The same thing happens to the "push" on rocks that starts at the earthquake's epicenter.

Earthquake waves are very complicated. Some waves travel through the Earth itself; others travel along the Earth's surface. Some waves move very rapidly; others move very slowly. By studying the different kinds of waves, scientists can determine where the earthquake's epicenter is and how deep it is located within the Earth.

The instrument scientists use to study earthquake waves is a *seismograph.* A seismograph consists of a heavy weight hanging from a spring or wire. When earthquake waves hit a seismograph, the dangling weight appears to jiggle up and down or back and forth. In reality, the weight does not move. It is the ground that moves up and down or back and forth, but to an observer, it looks like the weight is moving. Each kind of earthquake wave affects the seismograph in a different way.

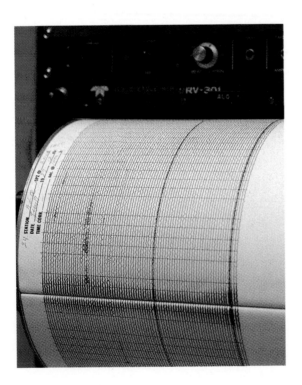

This seismogram shows the reading of a Nevada earthquake that registered 3.8 on the Richter scale.

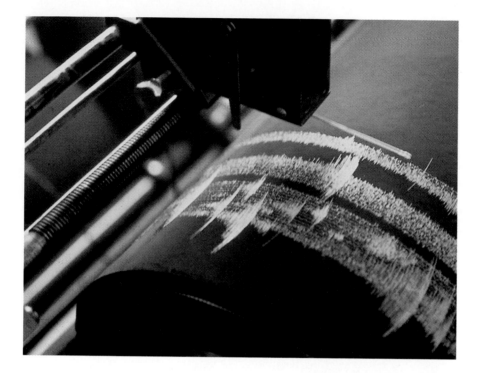

A seismograph at work.

The seismograph also contains a recording system. The recording system consists of a pen resting on a piece of paper. A motor very slowly moves the paper under the pen when the earth is still, the pen draws a straight line on the paper. But if the earth moves, the pen also moves in a jagged line. The more the earth moves, the more the pen jiggles, and the line become more jagged. The drawing made by the pen on a seismograph is called a *seismogram.*

Seismograms that have very high peaks and very low valleys come from the biggest earthquakes. Smaller earthquakes produce seismograms with smaller peaks and

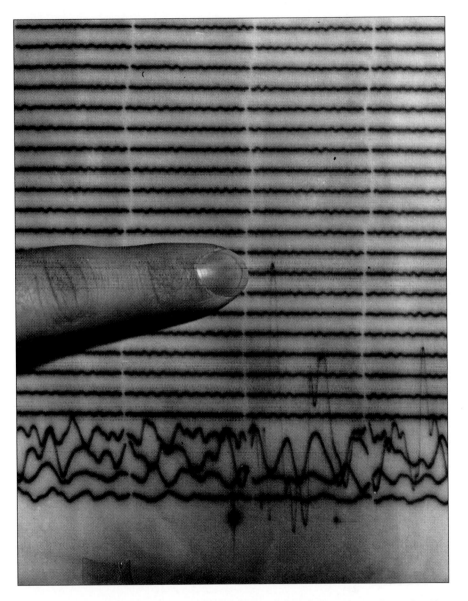

A scientist at the Fordham College Seismograph Station points out the high spot of an earthquake recording.

valleys. In the 1930s, an American *seismologist* (a scientist who studies earthquakes), Charles F. Richter, decided to measure the peaks and valleys on a seismogram. That measurement would tell how large or small an earthquake was. This was the first step in developing what we now know as the Richter scale.

One problem Richter encountered in developing his system is that the largest earthquakes are millions of times more severe than the smallest ones. His scale would have to use numbers from one (for small earthquakes) to more than a million (for large earthquakes). Richter thought that would be inconvenient.

Instead, he decided to use a special form of mathematics known as *logarithms.* In the logarithm system, the number *6* means ten times as much as the number *5.* So the peaks on a *6* seismogram are ten times as high as those on a *5* seismogram. The *6* seismogram also has peaks that are one hundred times *(10 x 10)* as high as the ones on a *4* seismogram. By using logarithms, Richter avoided having to use numbers in the millions, instead, he found he could measure earthquakes on a sacle of *1* to *10.*

The Richter scale also tells how much energy is released in an earthquake. An earthquake that measures 6 on the Richter scale releases 32 times as much energy as one that measures *5.* The same quake also releases one thousand times *(32 x 32)* as much energy as one that measures *4.*

The strongest earthquakes ever measured are *9* or more on the Richter scale. The 1906 San Francisco earthquake was estimated to have been *8.3* on the Richter scale. The 1989 earthquakes measured to be *7.1.*

A 1966 photograph of Dr. Charles F. Richter, who developed the first magnitude scale for earthquakes–the Richter Scale.

Fires billow over the Ginza District, Tokyo, Japan, 1923.

Victims of the fires in the Tokyo earthquake.

Notable Earthquakes of the Twentieth Century

1923 Tokyo and Yokohama, Japan.
An earthquake lasts five minutes. It starts fires and a tidal wave. Two-thirds of Tokyo is destroyed. More than 140,000 people are killed.

1949 Tadzhikistan, USSR
An earthquake sets off a rockslide. The village of Khait is buried in the slide. About 12,000 people are killed. The quake registers 7.5 on the Richter scale.

1958–1963 Lake Kariba, Zambia
More than 2,000 earthquakes occur. They are caused by the construction of a new dam. The most powerful are 5.8 on the Richter scale.

1960 Chile
The most powerful earthquake ever recorded. It reached 9.5 on the Richter scale.

1964 Anchorage, Alaska
One of the strongest earthquakes ever measured. It scored 9.3 on the Richter scale.

1973   Fukui, Japan
The city is destroyed. About 3500 people are killed. Richter scale reading of 7.3.

1980   Central Italy
An earthquake leaves 300,000 people homeless.

Other systems for measuring earthquakes have been suggested. The Italian seismologist Giuseppe Mercalli invented a system in 1902 using numbers from *1* to *12.* The Richter system measures how much energy is released in an earthquake. The Mercalli system measures how much damage the earthquake does. These two measures can be very different.

For example, an earthquake measuring *6.9* on the Richter scale hit Armenia on December 7, 1988. A Richter reading of *6.9* is not especially large, but this earthquake caused terrible damage. Hundreds of buildings were destroyed, and more than 25,000 people were killed. By comparison, a very strong earthquake hit the less-populated Aleutian Islands in 1957. It registered *9.1* on the Richter scale, but caused almost no damage to property or lives since there are few buildings on the island.

The Mercalli system uses changes that anyone can see. For example, here are some of the events that occur in a *4* Mercalli earthquake:

1. Some people are awakened from their sleep.

2. Dishes are moved around, but not broken.

3. Walls make a cracking sound.

4. Cars rock back and forth.

To use the Mercalli system, scientists send out questionnaires. They ask questions such as:

1. Were windows broken?

2. Were dishes broken?

THE MERCALLI SCALE

1. Felt by only a very few people.

2. Felt by a few, on upper floors.

3. Similar to a passing vehicle.

4. Felt by many people indoors.

5. Buildings tremble and trees shake.

6. Felt by all. Plaster cracks.

7. Bricks loosen. Difficult to stand.

8. Damage to weak structures.

9. Pipes crack. Buildings collapse.

10. Huge ground cracks. Landslides.

11. Most buildings destroyed.

12. Tsunamis. Total destruction.
    Surface waves seen.

3. Did walls crack?

4. If so, how big were the cracks?

Based on answers to these questions, scientists assign a Mercalli number to an earthquake.

The Mercalli number is different for different areas. Places close to the epicenter will experience more damage than those farther away. They will have a higher Mercalli number.

Using the Mercalli system, the highest score given in the 1989 San Francisco earthquake was a *9.* This score means that in areas near the epicenter, underground pipes broke, buildings fell off their foundations, and some buildings collapsed.

5

PREDICTING EARTHQUAKES

Earthquakes can cause terrible destruction, but the damage to lives and property would not be so bad if people knew when one was coming. If you knew to expect an earthquake in your town tomorrow, you could move away. You could take some valuable belongings with you. Buildings might be destroyed, but lives could be saved. So for many years, people have been trying to find ways to predict earthquakes.

There are some "folk" methods of predicting earthquakes. Many people believe that animals can sense an earthquake before it actually happens. Horses become frightened. Mice and rats leave their holes. Chickens fly from their nests. Dogs bark and run around. Fish swim wildly in ponds.

There may be other natural signs of earthquakes too. The skies may suddenly become dark and stormy. Or bright colors may light up the sky. Ponds and lakes may become muddy. Gas bubbles out of the water.

For years, ordinary people have used the these signs to predict earthquakes. They watch animals, the sky, and the water.

Scientists have simple explanations for some of these

phenomena. Animals have a better sense of feel than humans. Perhaps they feel very weak earthquake waves (or hear the sound waves) before humans do. Also, muddy ponds may be caused by gases escaping from the Earth.

The Chinese government has tried to use these signs to predict earthquakes. In the 1970s, it taught people to watch for changes in animal behavior and to keep an eye on lakes, ponds, and wells.

The government also used scientific instruments. It built 250 seismograph stations. More than 100,000 people were trained to measure earth movements. Thousands of reports were sent to a central office every day.

Then, early in 1974, signs began to warn of an earthquake. Everyone watched animals, ponds, and the sky very carefully. Seismogram readings were studied carefully. On February 4, a warning went out to Liaoning Province. Everyone had to leave their homes. An earthquake was expected very soon.

The prediction was correct. A terrible earthquake struck that day on the 4th. Many buildings were destroyed, but only a few people were killed. The system had worked! Had the Chinese found a way to predict earthquakes?

Unfortunately not. Less than two years later, China was hit by another earthquake. The quake struck near Tangshan City in July 1976. It was one of the worst in centuries. It reached *8.0* on the Richter scale, and up to 750,000 people may have died. But the Chinese government, however, said nothing about the disaster to the outside world. It was embarrassed that its prediction system had failed. Except for its single success in 1974, the Chinese system has not worked very well.

Modern scientists try to make two kinds of earthquake predictions: long-term and short-term. Long-term predictions are based on historical information. Suppose scientists know that earthquakes have occurred along the Jones Fault in 1830, 1880, 1930, and 1980. When do you think the next earthquake might occur there?

The earthquakes seem to happen about every fifty years. A good guess is that another earthquake will occur in about 2030.

But that kind of prediction is not very helpful. Suppose you live near the Jones Fault. Should you move away for the whole year of 2030? What if the earthquake comes a year early? Or a year late? What you really want is to know if an earthquake is coming next week. Or tomorrow.

Scientists try to predict an earthquake in the near future by measuring Earth movements along a fault. Records of these movements are kept over a long period of time. Scientists look for sudden changes in these records. A sudden change may stand for a *foreshock.* A foreshock is a minor quake that occurs minutes, hours, or days before a main earthquake.

So far, scientists have not found out how to recognize a real foreshock. They can't tell the difference between a foreshock and harmless ground movements. They only know a foreshock has occurred *after* the main earthquake has taken place. They hope someday to learn to recognize a foreshock *before* the main quake hits.

One of the instruments scientists use to study more about foreshocks is a simple instrument called the *tiltmeter.* A tiltmeter is nothing more than a long pan of water. The pan is placed across a fault. Suppose one side of the fault

SEISMOGRAPH: AN INSTRUMENT
THAT WRITES A PERMANENT
CONTINUOUS RECORD OF EARTH
MOTION A SEISMOGRAM

HELICORDER RV-301

OAKLAND

SAN
FRANCISCO

HAYWARD FAULT

3,000,000 PEOPLE

SAN JOSE

200,000 PEOPLE

LOMA PRIETA
SEGMENT

SANTA
CRUZ

WATSONVILLE

REGIONS
OF MOST
INTENSE
SHAKING

0   20 MILES

Earthquake prediction is especially important in California where
millions of people are at risk.

moves upward. The water in the tiltmeter flows from one end of the pan to the other. Scientists can measure this water movement. They can tell how much the earth has moved.

An *extensometer* measures back and forth and up and down movements. It consists of a very long rod laid across a fault. It acts like a yardstick measuring the distance between two points on the earth. Suppose the two sides of the fault move toward each other. The two points on the earth move closer to each other. The extensometer records this movement.

Earthquake scientists monitor readings around the clock.

Technicians use "wet" tiltmeters to measure gradual shifts in the Earth's surface by noting how the level of water in a pan tilts. These measurements help scientists in their difficult task of predicting when earthquakes might occur.

Lasers that beam across fault lines help detect movement in the earth. Scientists know the ground has shifted when the laser beam passes through the glass at an angle other than 90°. Here, a helium neon laser passes at the proper angle (the two reflected beams is a result of reflections off the front and back surfaces of the glass plate).

Earth positions can also be measured with laser light. A laser and a detector are set up on one side of a fault. A mirror is set up on the other side. Light goes from the laser to the mirror and then back to the detector. Suppose one side of the fault moves. Then the light will not be reflected in exactly the same way it was before. Scientists can measure how much the earth moved.

Even satellites are used in earthquake prediction. Instruments in the satellites can measure the position of continents. They can tell how much continents move each year, even if the changes are as small as an inch a year.

Instruments like these give scientists lots of numbers to work with. But what do these numbers mean? So far, not very much. Scientists have never predicted a single major earthquake. No one can guess how soon before they will be able to do so.

6

PREPARING FOR AN EARTHQUAKE

Charlotte could not believe her ears. The church bells were ringing! But it wasn't Sunday. The church bells normally rang only on Sunday.

Charlotte had no way of knowing that an earthquake was making the bells ring. The earthquake took place more than 1,000 miles (1,609 km) away from her home in Richmond, Virginia. The quake's epicenter was near the town of New Madrid, in the state of Missouri!

The New Madrid earthquake of 1811 has an important lesson today. Missouri does not lie on the boundary between two plates. It lies in the middle of a continental plate. No volcanoes are nearby. Who would expect an earthquake in Missouri?

Yet several have taken place. The 1811 quake could be felt not only in Richmond, but all along the Eastern coast. Many buildings around New Madrid were destroyed. The shape of the land was changed. But the earthquake caused few deaths and injuries because few people lived in Missouri in 1811. If another earthquake hit Missouri today, the story would be very different. More than ten million people live in the region, and buildings there are worth billions of dollars.

Another New Madrid earthquake could cause untold damage.

One lesson from the New Madrid earthquake is clear. Everyone should know about earthquakes. Maybe your town has never had a quake. But who knows what might happen in the future? What would *you* do if an earthquake struck?

For many people, this problem is very real. Millions of Californians live along the San Andreas fault. Millions more live along faults in Japan, China, India, Chile, Iran, and other nations of the world. Preparing for an earthquake is no imaginary game for these people. What can be done to protect life and property?

Japanese schoolchildren perform an earthquake preparation drill.

Hiding under a desk or sturdy table will help protect you from falling debris.

Children who live near faults often have a special class in school where they learn what to do in case of an earthquake. At school, students crawl under their desks to protect themselves from falling objects. Or, they may go to a safe part of the building. They practice for an earthquake the way all school children practice for a fire.

At home, people should stand in a doorway during an earthquake. The doorway protects them from falling walls and ceilings and is considered the safest place in the house.

Still, knowing these things may not help very much. People probably will not have any warning that an earthquake is coming. The best way to protect yourself is to prepare ahead of time for an earthquake.

The best preparation for an earthquake is to make buildings that can withstand earthquake shocks. In many parts of the world, houses are built of simple materials: mud, adobe, bricks, and wood. These materials are not very strong, so when an earthquake strikes, they collapse easily. For that reason, earthquakes in poor areas often result in many deaths.

Large buildings in earthquake zones are now built with special materials and special techniques. Steel rods are placed inside concrete for added strength. Some tall buildings ride on rubber tires that move back and forth during a quake. The buildings may move, but they will not fall down. The floors in such buildings are made of many sections. During an earthquake, some sections move upward, others move downward. The building vibrates, but floors do not break apart.

Homes can be made earthquake-safe too. One step is to bolt the house to its foundation. In the 1989 San Francisco earthquake, many houses slid off their foundations. Simply fastening a house to its foundation can prevent this accident. Chimneys can also be dangerous. They may break apart during an earthquake, however, a chimney reinforced with steel can survive most earthquakes.

Inside a house, a water heater can be a source of danger. The water heater may fall over during an earthquake, and the broken gas line can easily set the house on fire. The house might survive the quake but burn down from the fire.

Also think about your personal needs in case of an earthquake. Do you have a supply of food and water? Have you set aside a flashlight, a portable radio, and extra batteries? Do you know where to shut off the gas and water to your house? Are there fire extinguishers at hand? You will not have time for these preparations after an earthquake hits, so make sure you are ready ahead of time.

Earthquakes can cause terrible disasters, but wise preparation makes it possible for almost anyone to survive.

GLOSSARY

Epicenter —The point in the earth where an earthquake begins.

Extensometer — An instrument used to measure foreshocks; a long rod laid across a fault, measuring the distance and direction the ground has moved on either side of the fault.

Fault — The place where two moving plates of the Earth's crust push against each other, causing seismic activity and earthquakes.

Foreshock — A minor earthquake that occurs minutes, hours, or days before a main earthquake.

Logarithms — A mathematical system used to express numbers in a fashion different than simple counting. In logarithms, 6 means ten times as much as 5. This system is used in the Richter scale.

Meteorologist — A scientist who studies the weather.

Plates — Large pieces of the earth's crust that lie beneath the continents and oceans of the Earth's surface. The United States, Canada, and Mexico lie on the North American Plate.

Richter scale — Developed by seismologist Charles F. Richter in the 1930s; a system for measuring how much energy is released by earthquakes, using a logarithmic scale of 1 to 10.

Seismograph — The instrument used to detect, study, and measure earthquakes.

Seismogram — The line drawn by a seismograph, measuring the intensity of earthquakes.

Seismology — The area of science that studies earthquakes and seismic activities. Scientists who specialize in this area are called seismologists.

Tiltmeter — An instrument used to study foreshocks of earthquakes; a long pan of water placed across a fault; scientists measure how much water flows from one side to the other to determine how much the earth has moved.

Tsunamis — Tremendous waves caused by landslides occurring on the ocean floor during earthquakes.

FOR FURTHER READING

British Museum, Geological Department Staff. *Earthquakes.*
New York: Cambridge University Press, 1986.

Dudman, John. *The San Francisco Earthquake.* New York:
Franklin Watts, 1988.

House, James & Bradley Steffens. *San Francisco Earthquake.*
San Diego: Lucent Books, 1989.

Knapp. Brian. *Earthquake.* Austin, Texas: Steck-Vaughn, 1990.

Poynter, Margaret. *Earthquakes: Looking for Answers.* Hillside,
New Jersey: Enslow Publishers, 1990.

INDEX

ABOUT THE AUTHOR

David Newton is a prolific writer of science books for children and an award-winning teacher. He has written several chemistry, physics, and biology textbooks, as well as dozens of other books on virtually every science subject, including the wetlands, environmentalism, nutrition, population, AIDS, and sexuality. Mr. Newton's recent books for Franklin Watts include *Scientific Instruments, Taking a Stand Against Environmental Pollution, Consumer Chemistry Projects for Young Scientists,* and *Hunting.*